## As in Judy

Recently named 'literary hero' by *The Skinny*, Rosie is an award-winning poet, novelist and singer with post-punk band The March Violets. With a passion for language nurtured by libraries, she started out in spoken word, garnering praise from Apples and Snakes as 'one of the country's finest performance poets'.

Her firm belief in the power of persistence stems from personal experience. Following twelve years at a reputable literary agency (who failed to place her novels), she entered the 2011 Mslexia Novel Competition and won. This debut novel was published as *The Palace of Curiosities* (HarperCollins, 2013) and was nominated for both The Desmond Elliott and the Polari First Book Prize. Second novel, *Vixen* (Borough Press, 2014), was a Green Carnation Prize nominee. Her next novel, *The Night Brother*, is published June 2017.

GW00503610

*By the author*

*Poetry*

Hell and Eden [†•]

Coming Out at Night [†■]

Creatures of the Night [†■]

Things I Did While I Was Dead [★]

Everything Must Go [♦]

As in Judy [★]

*Novels*

The Palace of Curiosities [§]

Vixen [§]

The Night Brother [§]

[†] As Rosie Lugosi

Published by
[•]Dagger Press, [■]purpleprosepress, [★]Flapjack Press,
[♦]Holland Park Press, [§]HarperCollins Publishers

# Rosie Garland
## As in Judy

Flapjack Press
flapjackpress.co.uk

Published in 2016 by Flapjack Press
Chiffon Way, Salford, Gtr Manchester
flapjackpress.co.uk

ISBN 978-0-9955012-0-1

Author cover photograph: Leeds, c1982.
*Credit sought. Every effort has been made to trace the cover
photographer and obtain permission to reproduce this material.
Please do get in touch with any enquiries or any information
relating to this image or the rights holder.*

Printed by Imprint Digital
Upton Pyne, Exeter, Devon
imprintdigital.com

"You spend all that time trying to understand the world, its family relationships, friendships, social systems through a serial adventure of episodes mundane and or memorable. You spend all that time trying to fit into the human. Then, you are propelled into realisation through a life-threatening disease. Travelling not outward into the world but inward to the beating heart of the matter, you dive deep into the DNA. You are the resplendent there. You are the clicking queen of the insects. When you dress again in flesh and skin, you go amongst the sleeping humans and new and glittering worlds are left in your wake. Welcome to Rosie Garland!"

— John Hyatt

Heartfelt gratitude to Char March for her generous editorial input, which challenged me to make this a far tighter collection.

And to Ruth Fainlight, for her inspiring suggestion that 'As in Judy' would make a great title.

# Contents

Asking for Directions                                    11

*Queen of the Insects:*

When You Grow Up                                         15
My Favourite Uncle                                       16
Waving at Trains                                         17
First Night at Brownie Camp                              18
Gathered Here Today                                      19
Fast                                                     20
Belief Systems                                           21
Photograph of my Great-Grandmother                       22
Walking to Nine Ladies                                   23
Left. Right.                                             24
Still Life with Parrots                                  25
Cocaine Mummy                                            26
Peek-A-Boo                                               27
What Dreams May Come                                     28
Langsuyar                                                29
Dismantled                                               30
Eclipse – 11:08:1999                                     31
Personal Questions                                       32
The Ghost of You                                         34
Bug                                                      35
Funeral Songs                                            36
Breaking the Curfew with Dangerous Friends               37

*Flesh and Skin:*

| | |
|---|---|
| The Sum of All Meat | 41 |
| My Next Lover | 42 |
| One Night Stand | 43 |
| Long Goodbye | 44 |
| Fixing Punctures | 45 |
| Morphic Resonance | 46 |
| A Phase She Went Through | 47 |
| Redecorating the Bedroom | 48 |
| Wife of the Colonel | 49 |
| A Short History of Unicorns | 51 |
| Nursery Games | 52 |
| Strawberries | 53 |
| Mary of the Desert | 54 |
| Bacchus | 55 |
| Praise Song to the Buttocks | 56 |
| The Museum of Terrible Objects | 58 |
| Sir Thomas Aston at the Deathbed of his Wife | 59 |
| Pain Relief | 60 |
| The Sanctuary of Saints Cosmas and Damian | 61 |
| Confessional | 62 |
| Leaving the Moghul Paradise | 63 |
| Repairing Yorkshire | 64 |
| Departure Lounge | 65 |

*Syrinx:*

| | |
|---|---|
| Paint Strippers | 71 |

Some of these poems first appeared in the following publications:

*Ariadne's Thread, Bare Fiction, Best of Manchester Poets Vol. 3, Chicago Literati, Envoi, Fat Damsel, Freak Circus, Great Weather For Media, The Healing Muse, The Intima Journal of Narrative Medicine, Kulchur, The Lake, Lamplit Underground, Loose Muse, Melancholy Hyperbole, neo:writers, The North, Painted Bride Quarterly, Plenitude, Prole, Quaint, The Rialto, SAMPAD – Inspired By My Museum, Sculpted – Poetry of the North West, She's The One* and *Skin to Skin*.

Poems have also won or been placed in the following poetry competitions:

Angels and Devils, Ariadne's Thread, Exeter, Hippocrates, Manchester Cathedral, Salopian, SCJ, Ver and Wirral Festival of Firsts.

'Syrinx' was commissioned for the 2016 Wonder Women event at The Whitworth Art Gallery, Manchester.

## Asking for Directions

Take the road past the abandoned cliff-edge
hotel. A boy will lean out of a car and shoot
at you. Don't worry. He will miss. Follow

the bullet's breath to the hospital and its folded
wards. You imagine it is a dead-end. Continue
through its convoluted drainage system to a courtyard

with bricked-up doorways. Choose the only one
that's open, then along a bridle-path signed *no motor vehicles*,
past disbelieving wrecks of burnt-out trucks. Keep walking.

You'll arrive at the station breathless, too late
for your train and minus ticket, money, timetable. Stow
that ridiculously heavy suitcase in a locker and climb

the gravelled path up the hill. Yes, it gets steeper.
Your sat-nav? It won't work here. Feel your way
with the bravery you used to have when you crossed

roads without looking. Keep going. You can't miss it:
the sheer drop, the view back with its tarpaulin
of smoke, all those wooden markers.

*Queen of the Insects*

At night, she leaps and does not land. Spreads her arms and
    soars
above the fenced and neatly weeded garden. Her dreams
are practice sessions where she lifts cars, sees through walls,
    fights

dragons. She is a pirate captain, a queen, a horse. She is neither
    girl
nor boy: the distinctions are irrelevant when her small body
    encompasses
male and female; human, beast. A turbulent child figure-heading

the prow of her beaked ship, she buckles on armour, rescues
princesses from charming princes and spinning wheels.
She is fearless of the shapes beneath the bed. Too soon

she hears the summons: *Breakfast! Now!*
Blinks this world into focus. Hushes battle cries,
sheathes her sword between the pages of her book.

Every bedtime her mother tucks in
the sheet of marriage, husband, children: tucks it tight.

had tropical fish with sequinned jackets, suspended
above candied gravel; a mermaid with plastic breasts

who gargled bubbles. He had Auntie Brenda with her coiled
beehive and a mouth pursed for cigarettes. There was a magic

button in his Ford Cortina: when I pressed it, the light
in the vinyl roof came on. I was allowed to touch

his record player with its sapphire needle, the box of glossy
Top Ten 45s. He took me to burger bars with red twirling stools,

so tall my feet dangled. Taught me how to blow froth
in my milkshake. Laughed when the ketchup bottle farted.

He bought the perfect present: a tiny suitcase for my doll,
big enough for running away. I couldn't understand why

Brenda left him: left the fish, the car with its magic
switch, the songs, the gifts, the endless giggling.

On the bridge, I wave at every woman. Half the population
of Great Britain; thirty million according to Miss Grant.
A hundred women in each train, two trains on the way

to school, three on the walk home, makes five hundred;
times five days a week equals two thousand five hundred
which goes into thirty million too many times to work out.

I scratch the numbers in my notebook, string beads
of zeros across the bottom of each page to calculate how long
I've got to do this before I've waved to every single one.

Then I can be sure that one of them was her. The woman
who gave birth to me three thousand seven hundred
and twelve days ago, including leap years.

She will see something familiar in my hand,
read its semaphore, and know.

## First Night at Brownie Camp

I was late. Dad got lost, and I had to sleep
in the bell tent with Becky – who still wasn't speaking
to me – and a girl whose name I didn't catch.

I spread pages from yesterday's paper, dad's army trick
to keep you warm. The two girls giggled,
said I was too young to understand the joke.

The rest of the pack scoffed a midnight feast
in the main tent. I could hear their laughter.
The earth poked fingers though my sleeping bag.

I didn't know where the toilet was. Becky stayed asleep,
even when I asked the way. The other girl snored.
I lay awake. The wind got up. The tent swung

its skirt around the single wooden leg. It tugged
at the guy ropes, danced wilder as the rain blew in,
tearing at the pegs that held me down.

Everyone is pretending that they're trying not to cry.
Her father's mouth is stretched across his face
just like Monday mornings, when he shuts

his briefcase and leaves the house.
The men are wearing dull coats.
The women's hats are funny in that way

you're not allowed to laugh at. She hopes
her grandmother is wearing something more cheerful:
the cardigan with rabbit buttons

or the feathery slippers that tickle.
The minister's voice groans like a bee trapped
under the sink. Her grandmother read her

a story about the dunes at the heart of the Sahara;
how they make the same low moan when the wind blows
from the west. The books, the cardigan, the slippers

have all been packed away in brown cardboard boxes.
She wants to run home and take them out, one by one.

## Fast

Carol is in a hurry to get out
of her school uniform. She skips
last period (Biology: boring). On the back seat
she hoists her blazer as a screen, fingers fumbling
to unknot her tie, cheeks flushed
with Mary Quant blusher.

By the time the bus skids
into the turning circle next to Boots,
her skirt and sensible shoes are stripped, stowed,
swapped for satin flares and a flap-collared shirt.
She is first out of the swinging doors, racing
over the road to her apprentice-builder boyfriend:
grabs his half-smoked cigarette and sucks
it to the stub in one deep hectic gulp.

## Belief Systems

Swallowed chewing gum ties a knot
round your intestines, slowly choking your insides.
An apple pip is worse; plants a tree
that sprouts up your throat.
Babies come from cabbage patches.
If you dig a hole, and keep digging, you reach Australia.
If you step on pavement cracks a bear will eat you.
Collect a million bus tickets
and win a million pounds.
Wearing glasses makes you brainy.
Only girls with long blonde hair can play the Virgin Mary.
Those with dark hair are the sheep.
Jesus loves you. God is always watching.
Grown-ups are always right. You must
say *yes* nicely when they ask.
Baddies wear black hats.
Soldiers are brave. Don't talk to strangers.
Boys don't cry. Nice girls wear white socks.
Smoking makes you cool.
Kissing gets you pregnant.
When you lose your virginity your nipples turn brown.
You can't get pregnant the first time you do it.
It doesn't count if you do it standing up.
When ladies grow up they get married and have children.
Your boyfriend will love you forever and never leave you

if you just do what he wants.

## Photograph of my Great-Grandmother

In the teeth of her husband's death, she leans
on the cabinet with its ugly drawer-handles.

She strokes her neck, the last place he touched her.
Clutches a fan, snapped shut tight as an unwanted telegram.

She has never met my gaze. Stares out of the window
in the direction of Passchendale.

She left me the dark lace,
her far-off eyes, her determined chin.

He demands each detail of the walk: the splinter
of dried-out heather, the fly agaric clenched in crimson fists,
tea staled by the thermos, the gravelly biscuits.

His face hangs above the mottled bedspread, fingers fumbling
for loose threads in the weave to hang onto, haul
himself closer. His back hooks a question mark.

What we are not saying thickens, promising rain before evening.
If there were trees here, I could read the landscape: could track
my way back by the gaps between their outstretched arms,
the deep red wooden hearts of them, grounded.

## Left. Right.


Item: scuffed maple box with stiff upper lid.
No inscription; key missing.

Item: regimental button, face muddied.
Once polished to attention
every Friday; ranked next to brass brothers.

Item: khaki arms of jacket resting easy
over stiff-backed kitchen chair,
elbows worried threadbare.

Item: hand that shone the buttons, shouldered
the epaulettes, set the peaked cap to rights, buckled
the Sam Browne. Now gone to ground,
along with cap, belt, boots, swagger stick.

## Still Life with Parrots

Her rule; anything not worn for two years goes.
The bin bag gapes. She stuffs it
with sale bargains, tags still dangling:

the coat kept for a best which never came,
the stilettos that made her hobble,
a cashmere sweater lost to moths,

the gloves with ratted fake fur cuffs,
brooches missing half their stones,
a magpie nest of hairgrips

and a storm blue kimono, exploding
with a jungle of macaws, beaks yanked
wide. The fabric waterfalls

between her fingers, rips under its own weight.
Pulling free of the satin drag,
the birds flap, tearing their threads.

## Cocaine Mummy

She tilts her chin at our stares as we ghost
past her crisp glass coffin. She cricks her neck,
cracks the wrinkled grin of an old stoner
who scored massive and isn't telling where.

Her flattened dugs and gilded nipples
have been in and out of fashion
a hundred times, her shaved quim
also. She bares her teeth in a rustle

of laughter at the drone of our thousand thousand
questions, our rabbit-quick breath misting her window.

## Peek-a-Boo

You snip round your face, tell me to guess.
The blades suggest Red Riding Hood, sweetheart chin
and button nose. But what sharp teeth you have;
how they sieve each breath. What eyes; those slitted pupils.

You cut again, make yourself more reasonable
until you think I'm fooled. But you're no Snow White
and I'm onto you. The more I won't believe
in these fairy tales the nastier you get, threaten

wives stuffed and mounted on the hunter's wall,
my heart ripped out and chewed, spiked barrels,
three pigs belly-up on the butcher's slab.
You always were a prick.

I'm done with happy-ever-after.
I dance out of the forest in tight red slippers.

Too hot for bedsheets. The room pants swollen air.
He stands at the window, palm circling his stomach.

Under the rhododendron, a panther draws itself together
from the night, unravels claws across the grass.

He turns to his wife; her back a low wall along the mattress.
Her thighs twitch in that recurring dream of running.

When he looks round, the cat has gone, leaving a scatter
of pawprints the same size as the wine glass he left on the lawn.

He thinks he's too wound up to go back to sleep, but
next thing he knows, it's morning. There's an empty snarl

of sheets beside him. He stumbles downstairs. The kitchen
stinks of cat tray. He unlocks the back door, calls her full name

to the shorn grass, the stripped privet.
The shadows beneath the magnolia stir themselves, uncoil.

## Langsuyar

She combs her hair long, a black sheet
to cover the new mouth at the back
of her neck, where angry stories leak out.
At night, its whispers drag

her from her bed and into the heart
of the city. She grins a slice of moon.
Her new lips smack, demand
scarlet lipstick, wine, the sweet breasts

of women and the hearts of men.
She roars in alleyways, throws away
the keys, laughs loud as a bucket
hauled up from life's well.

Her prince comes. She needs rescue
from the witch's curse.
He carries knives to shear her hair
and ram it down her throat, deep.

## Dismantled

The neighbour's boy does things with wire
unravelled from the youth club fence. Barbs rip
his palms; scab over fast as a paving slab dropped
off a railway bridge. He staggers

between cars when the lights turn green, ignores
the screech of tyres, shouts of *you stupid little*—.
He spends the weekend stripping
down his dad's mobile phone, tests how far he can go

before it won't start again. Props a shoebox
on a stick, scatters crusts to trap
scabby pigeons. That old lady's cat
goes missing. His bike chain spilt

in sticky loops across the lounge carpet. His sister
unparcelled, to see what makes her tick.

## Eclipse – 18:08:1999

We put on the smoked glasses, so shadow-black
they smog the sun to a blip on the screen of the sky.

We drink beer. I toss peanuts, get one stuck.
You thump my back. *I saved your life*, you grin.

The sun is half gone now, slipping behind the dark thumbprint
of the moon. The afternoon thickens to evening.

I am not prepared for the spread of this malignant light
across the garden, the silence of our held breath.

## Personal Questions

*With thanks to 'Sure, you can ask me a personal question' by Diane Burns.*

No, I'm not a smoker. No, I never have been.
Yes, it's one that smokers get.
No, I'm not a heavy drinker. No, I never have been.
Yes, it's one that drinkers get.
Yes, you can say it's unfair.
No, I don't see it that way.

No, this isn't a punk haircut.
No, this isn't a perm.
No, it wasn't this curly before.
No, I don't want to wear a wig.
Yes, I could get one on the NHS. A pretty one. A good one.
No, I don't want to wear a scarf.
Yes, I could get one on the NHS. A pretty one. A good one.

No, I haven't tried multi-vitamins.
Or selenium.
Or coenzyme Q10.
Or folic acid.
Or beta-carotene.
Or coffee enemas.
Or broccoli.
Or linseed.
Or the Gershon technique.

Ah, so you have an aunt with cancer.
Ah, your brother.
Yes, it's the same as Michael Douglas.
Yes, things have moved on since you were a boy.

Yes, there's a better chance these days.
Yes, it's amazing what they can do.

Thanks for saying I look well.
No, I don't feel it.
No, I don't like it when you squeeze my hand.
Or hug me.
Or stroke my hair.
And say it's soft as a baby's.

Yes, these electric wheelchairs are useful.
Ah, so you think they're brilliant.
Ah, so you'd like one yourself to get about.

No, I don't think I'm brave.
Really, I don't see myself as brave.
No, really.
If you must, then.

No, there's nothing you can do for me.
No, there's nothing you can do.

## The Ghost of You

We are sisters in sickness, two chemo chicks.
Make jokes no one else can understand;
like *do you know who I am?*
because it's easy to lose sight of things
as small as names through the fog of narcotics.

We cheerlead each other through the sweats,
the sickness, the boredom, the thankless task
of grinding through those long weeks on the ward.
Hold quiet tickertape parades to celebrate
the tiniest gains in weight, or getting out of bed,
showered and dressed before midday.

We trade recipes for gentle custards, soups; rejoice
when we discover how to make tofu taste of something.
We teeter down our private catwalk
comparing scarves, hats, long-sleeved shirts
to cover tracklines left by the canula.
We giggle at the ugly prescription wigs;
go bald together, brave out the stares.

We invent new sports: One Hundred Metre Barfing
and Speed Waddling with Zimmer Frame.
We pant out our marathon. But when I breast
the yellow tape I turn to find you gone; your fire stamped out.

The path ahead is lonely.
Your memory sparkles. Your photographs still shine.

## Bug

For seven days I have not slept
more than an hour at a time; two on a good night.

Cocooned in tight sheets, I eavesdrop
the lullaby of the emergency lighting,

the shrieking wheels of the commode,
the machine that beeps my vitals every hour.

Night after wide-eyed night I'm defleshed
of the sine waves of dreaming that mark us *human*.

The nurse at the foot of my bed sighs,
flicks her pen along a line of boxes, strikes me from

her list of known mammals. De-classified, I drop off
the edge of this flat earth into a sleep of monsters

where dragons stretch their claws. I am no longer
mapped, safe. I lurch on insect legs, stripped

to an exoskeleton, the shrivelled thorax
of a wasp where my belly used to swell;

ribs tight as beetle wings, mouthparts clicking.
Dry hours whirr as I practise night vision

with composite eyes, smacking headlong over and over
into each flat clear morning, tough as plate glass.

I want the Kinks. Because they were cheerful,
grew their hair long (which is still boyish wild),
sang *Thank You For The Day* and I am thankful

for the grind of coffee incensing the stairs,
the hours it takes to simmer chicken soup,
the bronze of autumn sun gladdening the chimney,
rain scouring out the gutters. Clean, clean.

I want my ears to brim with Sandy Denny,
voice clear as a breaking heart.
*Who Knows Where The Time Goes.*
It's a tough question. Think it over.

There will come a time when we let slip our hold.
We'll be a long time quiet.
While we have breath, shout; taste fire.
Choose songs for then, sing them now.

## Breaking the Curfew with Dangerous Friends

Tonight, they are back in town,
lipstick scrawled on mouths strong from saying *No*.
They make quick work of roadblocks – *lady, baby,*
*bitch, witch, slut* – snap them like tinder-sticks.

They sneer at ranked telephoto lenses, stare down
those who gloat at the tabloid mess made of their bodies.
They stride to each house and knock:
not to help with the dishes or change

nappies, but to rouse us where we slump,
fretting over the bills, the buckled marriage,
the dinner party menu of impossible dishes.
Not all of us hear them. Some crank up

the volume on the TV, some swallow
themselves into computer screens. I ignored
them the last time they were here, laughed off
the warnings, thought of all the safe years stretching

out before me. This time my ears are cocked
for the gravel crunch of footsteps. I've slashed
the hemline of my skirt to show the muscles
I have built for running. My shoes are at the door.

*Flesh and Skin*

## The Sum of All Meat

He is mathematician: precise fractioner
of cows, pigs, lambs. He subtracts breath
from meat; calculates the angle where the blade
must intersect for perfect division: by two, by four,
apportioned into clod, rump, prime rib, brisket, loin.

Wives don't want details. But a split
side of beef is a wonder of solid geometry.
In its Rorschach bisection he sees angels
spread-eagling heavy wings; inhales their greasy breath.

At the close of this day's lesson, he will delay
the washing of his hands, inky
with the algebra of meat's beauty.

## My Next Lover

curls fingers round the chair back and pulls
it from under the table. Gestures me to sit;

flat wood inviting the print of my hips, thighs.
Cups a hand round the curve

of a wine glass; slow swirl of bloody liquid.
The skin beneath my breast flushes

at the press of lips. Not yet: in a few hours.
The mouth of my next lover moves

in snatches of conversation. I lean forward
to catch each word. The wet glitter

of teeth, lilac flicker of tongue. I tip
my head and laugh. Not at the jokes –

although they are good jokes –
but at the drag of a hand at the nape of my neck,

that will grasp and pull back, tonight.

## One Night Stand

I cross the road to see the other side,
leave map and torch behind,
thinking the bright light of my smile
will be enough to get me through.

The dance moves are identical,
songs have the same saccharin words.
I spend the remainder of the night trying
to retrace my steps, stomach growling from lack of food.

## Long Goodbye

You can't sleep. It's not his snoring, or the fog
of stale wine, but the latest late-night argument.
This time, how much a freelance artist should kowtow
to the client: you (a lot), him (never). You tick off

the small hours, replaying every line
and crafting perfect answers, pointless now,
until 6am and the bells start ringing
Sunday in. You creep to the shower, sluice

off more than duvet sweat. Sun pounds
on the filthy kitchen window. You're polite
through coffee and defrosted croissants;
shoes laced, bag zipped shut and waiting

at the back door. You drive west with a clean
morning behind you, lighter with each mile;
over Saddleworth where the tarmac splits
round that stubborn farm. He calls. You don't answer.

He leaves a message: *I've found your house keys
on the bathroom floor, your favourite t-shirt underneath the bed.*

## Fixing Punctures

I say, *it's my fault*. Repeat three times, till
her face softens and I know the words have sunk in.
*I'll always love you*, I add, waiting for the smile
that makes things better. I say I'll fix
a chilli for dinner, homemade guacamole,
my famous salsa with tomatoes just past ripe.

I hold the door; tip my chin for the kiss and she's off.
All through the breakfast dishes I think how
this will blow over. I go to the wholefood store, pricey
but the only place with scotch bonnets; select
an avocado, thumb its belly for softness.

I imagine her at the bike co-op, hands slippery
with grease: stripping down, rebuilding bikes from scratch.
She is fixing punctures for lazy cyclists; holding
the inner tube under water and watching
the stream of bubbles rise in a delicate silver chain.

## Morphic Resonance

In Yorkshire and Australia, sheep lie down;
roll across cattle grids,
plastic ear tags clicking on the steel.

I turn over on the stretched springs of my mattress.
Across the Pennines you twist
in her bed, bleat my name.

## A Phase She Went Through

You write to say you're happy now, better
since you ditched smoking and took up Pilates.
You and the American – the one with the huge
inheritance – have produced a son called Josh.

You take fortnights in the Maldives. You never think
of that weekend in Whitby, and have thrown out
that photo of us in ripped fishnets, dancing uncontrollably
to the only cheerful record by The Cure.

## Redecorating the Bedroom

Dig out the steamer from underneath
the stairs, fill the reservoir, plug it in and wait
for it to seethe, pant hot air. Press
its humid mouth against the wall, shove
the steel tongue into wrinkled woodchip and strip

the room naked. Scrape through strata of Anaglypta
and blown vinyl to plaster pockmarked
with picked-off scabs. Dribble
flabby glue onto the boards. Watch paper pile
against the skirting board in a heap of dropped knickers.

Roll and dump the carpet, so you never
have to tread old footsteps. Shuffle
swatches of Berber, Wilton, cut pile, twist.
Choose new ground beneath your feet.

## Wife of the Colonel

*In 1929, Colonel Victor Barker was tried at the Old Bailey and imprisoned for 'impersonating a man and entering an illegal marriage' with Elfrida Howard.*

In cross-examination, you insist
I must have been complicit; alert
to his transgressive nature.

My Lord, I am a lady
and a lady does not question
her spouse's excess of modesty.

In nuptial matters,
a lady does not know
there are questions to be asked.

In after-dinner stories about shooting
(grouse, duck, stag or Hun) he matched the best of them
for tedium. My upright man,

back to the fire:
boot-black hair, the firm press
of his trouser-crease.

You will have it that I am deluded.
Or debauched. Or desperate.
You jut your chin, expect me to fudge and fumble.

*Pax, magister.* I clench my fists inside their gloves. He
(or *she*, as you are insisting)
was the perfect husband. A natural gentleman.

There are tales I will never tell in my defence:
the slow interrogation of his hands,
the way my body answered.

She could never swear to it: it happened fast.
4am, every taxi flying past; staggering home
down blank streets of doors that weren't hers,
a slop of vodka and Red Bull curdling her insides.

The whisk of its tail flicking moths as it lifted
its face from the ripped gut of the bin bag
and tiptoed across the road, nostrils curious.
The nib of its rippled horn drew a line

of blood across her stomach as it butted
its nose into the fork of her thighs. The smell
rising from its head, like the baby
when her sister let her hold him. Mascara dripped

off her chin. She wanted to say sorry
for the stink of her breath, her armpits,
for all the fucking, all the fucking up,
how she hadn't been the one to cock

and fire the gun at the last Javan tiger,
the last Tasmanian wolf. The beast opened
its mouth: the salt coil of its tongue as it slid
across her face, between her lips.

## Nursery Games

She hides
in the thicket of shadows
under the stairs, tucked
behind the shabby hedge of coats,
the long-boned broom
and the mop nesting its claws in a bucket.

She bites
her tongue, hooks fingernails
into her palm. It hurts less
than the end of bedtime stories.

She wants
to be as small as a cup handle
you cannot push your finger through.

One day
she will escape
in the stomach of a giant fish,
like Sister Bernadette's story
of the man who was patient.

She counts back
from one hundred,
holding onto the sneeze
that is swarming her nose with wasps.

She is listening
for his key screeching in the lock,
for tonight's game
of *coming, ready or not.*

## Strawberries

My mother buys packs of Kotex
the size of pillows, leaves them
on my bed. I don't open them.
Don't want to talk, however often she screws up
her forehead and tips her head
to one side, like her neck's been snapped.

I'm the only one in class without this excuse
to get off cross-country. I skip lunch, pound
my body round the track while they sneak
cigarettes and gasp as Sharon coughs up
every sticky detail of doing it with Rob from Year 11.

School Nurse says some girls are late developers.
*But I wasn't,* says mum and her eyes do that thing,
how she's afraid for me. How I'm not
a real woman: one who swells into hothouse fruit, huge
but flavourless; like those strawberries we got
at Christmas. I held them under running water,
twisted off the green stems, fingers stained with juice.

## Mary of the Desert

For twenty years she prayed
to be whittled to a twig,
all sap sucked out;
to be a flapping wallet
upturned and penniless.

God answered
through the bodies of beasts.

An ox peeled off its hide
and made a tent to shade her burning breasts.

An eagle plucked itself to pimples
and heaped quills beneath her head.

A lion wiped her feet with his sweaty mane;
a snail anointed her toenails with silver.

That evening, she dined on steak tartare;
danced the hootchie-kootchie
flicking a dove-feather fan.

## Bacchus

*From Michelangelo's statue in the Bargello, Florence.*

My thighs slump. Last night is a twelve hour lacuna
of boozing, puking, and boozing again. Thumbprints
off some other drunk blot the marble slick of my stomach,
the trodden doormat of my arse. My cock
sucked away by a mouth that missed the glass.
Some bastard has twisted thorns round my head.
When I get hold of him, I swear.

Come a bit closer. There are two of you.
I can still heft a pint, you see?
Look at my balls. Fucking look at them.

## Praise Song to the Buttocks

Oh, heads of newborn twins!
Identical, monozygotic; you smile deep, vertical,
hamster-cheeked above the velvet twist of the anus,
dumb-bells bench-pressed by the thighs.

Oh, breasts reversed!
balancing behind what thrusts before.
My coco-de-mer, dolphin backs that gleam
when cresting ocean.

I cannot appreciate my own swell;
rely on mirror glimpses, neck-twisting and reassurances.
So I am greedy in you, double instruments of my passion.

Let me lay down upon your cushions, rock in your lovers' seat,
button-backed and peach-leathered, dimpled velvet.
There is nothing more delicious than your curve
when I lean into you.
Soft valley, warm vale of earth,
my hands stroll your hills, glut on your tang of earth and salt.

Oh, cumulonimbus heaped around the eye of the storm!
Oh thunderclap of hands!
You are famous for raucous language.
Your nether mouth blurts earthy humours:
Bronx cheer and trumpeting brass section.
You are the punch line to limericks and riddles.

You are my treasure sacks, my pirate booty.
Kneaded dough left overnight to bloom,

winter-warm beneath the blanket. You are crumpets, muffins,
humped buns split and greased with butter;
rump steak, pancake, shimmy shake and jelly-wobble.
Horns of plenty, I dine on you.

Cheek to cheek you rise from the mattress,
orbit the bed like sun and moon on the fourth day of creation.
I am not your God. I am a candle raised
to praise your best angle.
Swing low, sweet Io, sweet Europa!
In the stroking of you I have found out the rotation of planets.
In the kissing of you I have discovered electricity.
You are excellent in gravity;
the *ow* in *wow*, my one-eyed kingdom.

There is nothing sweeter than your mastery in grasping:
for you can hold a coin, a hand, and all my secrets.

## The Museum of Terrible Objects

A lifetime of clipped toenails, reattaching to the toe.
A sheep that bleats the works of Shakespeare
in Morse Code. Today, the Comedies.

A jar of starving wasps.
The ghosts beneath your bed formed into fists.
A dog in a breathless car.

A grain of rice carved with *Help!* in fourteen languages.
A child in a bottle, bubbles rising to the cork.
The quiet space behind your chair.

A television whispering and only you can hear.
The name of the Unknown Soldier.
The answer to the question *Why?*

This is Hall One of fifty-nine.
No one is allowed to leave
until they have purchased items from the gift shop.

## Sir Thomas Aston at the Deathbed of his Wife

*From the painting in Manchester Art Gallery.*

I reel to a tumult of voices. Laughing
or wailing, I can not tell.

My collar is too tight, the string
of my cuff knotted into a lump

by unquiet fingers. I am off kilter,
as though the artist was a drunkard.

Her face is grey as my beard; hand paler than my shirt.
Her blood has been given to the bed.

## Pain Relief

He walks wide-eyed into the ocean, pulls
the waves over his head and dives
into the slop of the kraken's gut.
He sits motionless, in case he sticks
in the whale's craw and is spat back home.

Its innards rumble in salty fermentation.
Despite the smell, he swills the slimy beer.
Glugs pint after pint, till he can't hear the thunder
of dry fists against the belly of the beast,
the cries of his rescuers, bellowing his name.

## The Sanctuary of Saints Cosmas and Damian

This morning, Saint Pantaleone is lazy sludge in his bottle
so we climb to Ravello, punish our legs
with steps hacked into the mountain. I lose count
after two hundred, and still the path staggers up the hill.
I'm breathless with apology; lug guilt at forcing this pilgrimage.

The church squeezes its shoulder under a jut of volcanic rock.
In its shelter glints a greenhouse of milagros, nailed
to velvet that is juicy with mould. Amputated
feet, arms, heads, disembodied hearts
and a tarnished photo of Paulo in case God
should confuse his parts with those of another.

A nun gives me bread as hard as bone. In the body
of the church the faithful embrace, hymn greetings.
The saints puff out breastplates windowed with relics,
flash gold teeth through soldered grins;
patient at the unending moans about bad luck,
bad backs, broken homes, stabbing pains.
Over my head, mosaic glitters miracles.
The risen dead cough dust. See! They walk. They dance.

## Confessional

The Madonna swam up the estuary, face flat
on a snapped plank. He waded in, mud sucking

his ankles, hauled her out like you would a stuck lamb.
The priest said she was a piece broken off an Old Master,

but he knew a holy virgin when he saw one. He polished
off the dirt, begging her pardon as he wiped.

Her lips swelled against his hand, cheeks bulged
with the secrets the angel brought from god and stuffed

between her teeth. Her eyes tickled his palm.
He propped her next to his bed and lay awake listening

to the wood clicking as it dried, the sound of a woman sucking
her tongue. He pressed his cheek to hers, felt the wood fluttery

with breath. In the morning he ran for the priest, begged him
to lock her in the church with the other miraculous things.

## Leaving the Moghul Paradise

You have shoved one foot outside
the burnished frame of Eden, into the blank gape
of the margin. Your toes pat vellum, feel for solid ground.
An angel with a primped mouth bars your return.

At your back, vines climb the page in jewelled knots,
the laboured calligraphy of God. Cherubim hammer
the night into a furnace of hosannas. You can't sleep,
can't think, can't love in the swarm of heaven.

You are searching for parchment without ink,
unscored by iron lines. Your own book,
where words have not yet been decided.
Uninscribed, unwritten, unbound, open to translation.

# Repairing Yorkshire

*First you have to dismantle it. No point trying*
*to plug holes willy-nilly.* The stones turn
green cheeks to the surprise of October sunlight.

He bends, shaved head russet from the lifting,
sweater snagged at the right wrist and unravelling.
He cradles each boulder it as you might a baby.

Over the Calder Valley the sky changes in the space
of moments. The man crinkles his eyes
as a cloud shaped like an anvil hammers the horizon.

An unpacked six foot stretch of dry stone wall. Each laid out,
ready to be set right. To either side, the wall collapses
in a litter of toppled markers, as far as he can see.

# Departure Lounge

After breakfast I take the bus to Terminal 2.
Not to fly away, but to leave last night behind:
the sting of disinfectant, the raucous trolleys,
the light parching your scalp.

I've come to join those eager to be gone;
where leaving is longed for and return is a dirty word.
Suitcases piled on baggage carts are crammed
for perfect getaways that keep the brochure's promise.

The twang of their excitement draws lines in the air
from wristwatch to departure board and back.
They fan themselves with boarding cards,
fingers crossed against the words *flight cancelled*.

You left at 3am, while the night was still licking
its lips. Your final destination is not listed
alongside Alicante, Palma, Arrecife. The tests
said up to a year. I hoped you had a longer stay;

prayed for delays. Joined a conspiracy
of forgetting that there was no time left at all.
The departure screens unfurl red flags.
Please proceed directly. Final call. Gate closed.

*Syrinx*

On 3rd April 1913, three suffragettes – Annie Briggs (48, housekeeper), Evelyn Manesta (25, governess) and Lillian Forrester (33, married, occupation not given) – entered Manchester Art Gallery. They attacked a specific group of paintings, including 'The Last Watch of Hero' (tragic female waits for brave lover), 'Captive Andromache' (tragic female mourns for brave lover), 'Astarte Syriaca' and 'Sybilla Delphica' (two examples of dyspeptic female as muse).

They also attacked 'Syrinx' (Arthur Hacker, 1854).

A lesser-known story from Ovid's *Metamorphoses*, Syrinx is one in the snaking line of spoiled-goods females transformed from human into *thing*. Other examples include Daphne into a tree, Io into a cow. Syrinx was changed into reeds to escape being raped by the god Pan. Who proceeded to fashion a set of pipes from the reeds, so he could forever press his lips and blow. Keep her hung around his neck.

'Syrinx' is still hanging in her gallery, ironically (or not so much) entitled 'The Pursuit of Beauty'. All these Bluebeard wives, nailed to the wall: bruised lips, bruised eyes, blurred quims and breasts like cakes.

Follow Annie, Lil and Evie as they run ring-a-rosie round the gallery, swinging toffee hammers...

## Paint Strippers

I

Listen. Tap of cloven heels across the floor.
Goat breath sweats your skin from ear to collar tip.
Scratch of beard between your shoulder blades.

Look, he bleats. Look what I've got. Come close.
Lean across the red rope and take your turn.
Go on. The breath of her last watcher fogs her thighs,
dripping syrup. You're next.
Add your gaze to the white noise hiss of a thousand years.
Nothing wrong with looking. They can't touch you.

No one is being hurt. She's not real. She's oil on canvas.
Pigment. Wormholes. A few swipes of a tarry brush.
Still trotting out that horny goat-boy trope?
This is Greek. The classics. It's got gravitas. It's got culture. *High.*

Shh now. Don't make waves.
Lie back and lose yourself in water.
Be new Ophelia, pillowed on pretty flowers.
This will be over, soon.
Imagine: a quiet life, a liquid life,
never getting in the way. Never
taking up more than your allotted space.
To fit any shoe given you, and fit it to perfection.

## II

Syrinx cannot make this any simpler. She hates this, always has.
She is no odalisque, spread as a willing dish.
We know what terror looks like, when a woman's saying no.
When she's trying to escape the paint that glues her to canvas,
that dissolves her clothes in turpentine.
Oils away her pubic bush.

All she wants is five minutes respite from the gawp.
We will not let her be. Syrinx is sick of it,
of trying to drag these reeds around her
and fight off a rogue's gallery of justifications.
Too right she's scowling.
She's had it up to here with being Muse,
plot point, trope, meme. Lost in the welter.
Sick of the painted-into-the-corner game,
the Venus-in-her-shell game.

## III

Syrinx has had a hundred lifetimes to reconsider.
She digs in her elbows, clenches fists.
Grasps the bars of her frame and rocks
till it shivers, thumps the wall.
The joints unjoint, crash to the floor.
Varnish cracks, glass jigsaws
in a rattling percussion of escape.

She shakes sawdust from her hair
and... Stretches. Stands
taller than any drink-me potion girl.
Spreads her arms and fingertips the walls.
What big arms she has!
All the better for spanning centuries.
What big thighs!
All the better for getting off her knees.
What big shoulders!
All the better for hefting the roof beam like a yoke
and splintering its matchstick.

No room can hold this new goliath. She breaks
the glass dome ceiling, knuckle-cracks the windows.
hangs earring chandeliers and wears the gallery
like a coat of many-coloured terracotta. Buttons up the bricks.
Makes boots of display cases, kicks over every pedestal.

She rips up the cards that mis-name her sullen, coquette, myth.
Spits out every word. Fuck flirtatious.
Fuck tasteful nude. Fuck temptress.

Enough of this mislabelling as amorous pursuit,
as if rape is a game of kiss-chase.
Skirting round what happens when skirts are torn away.
Fuck shifting goalposts. Fuck being seen and not heard.

Syrinx takes her first unfettered step. And another, another,
pounds Oxford Road. Picks up speed,
shedding plaster, paint, mortar,
a century and a half of sticky eyes.

Crushes roadblocks, hurdles, scholarship apologies. She skips
the pewter tightrope of the Ship Canal to Liverpool and leaps.
Parts waves, skims ocean.
Makes a road, broad enough to follow.


# IV


They say there are only seven plots. Seven ways to speak a life.
It's in the way we tell our own. She's told hers.
She's made her way and it's up to us to make our own.
This is a fight that's never done. One inch forward, half back.
And –
you can make **some** of the women hate themselves **all** of the time
and **all** of the women hate themselves **some** of the time,
but you can't make **all** women hate themselves **all** of the time.

Here is a candle to light up your head.
Here is a hammer to break up your bed.
Brick by little brick bring down the house that Jack built.
Roar loud enough to strip paint. Scrape lies from canvas.
Demolish the walls we've built around our dreams.
We've slept too long. Blamed pricked fingers, magic mirrors,
castles overgrown with thorns.
Time to unpick the one-size-fits-all answers
and weave new stories, complete
with dropped stitches, ragged hems.

Time. To open our eyes and learn to stare back.
Lay down the mirrors of others' lies. Be our own gods.
Make art of ourselves the way we choose:

fat, thin, hairy, young, old,
in one piece or in millions, cracked and crazed.

There is the road of our own life to walk
and our own shoes to walk it in.
Take back our day, our night. String new constellations:
the freak, the bitch, the witch, the harridan.
The road travelled. The life lived.
The room of one's own. The book waiting to be written.
The Dance. The Song.